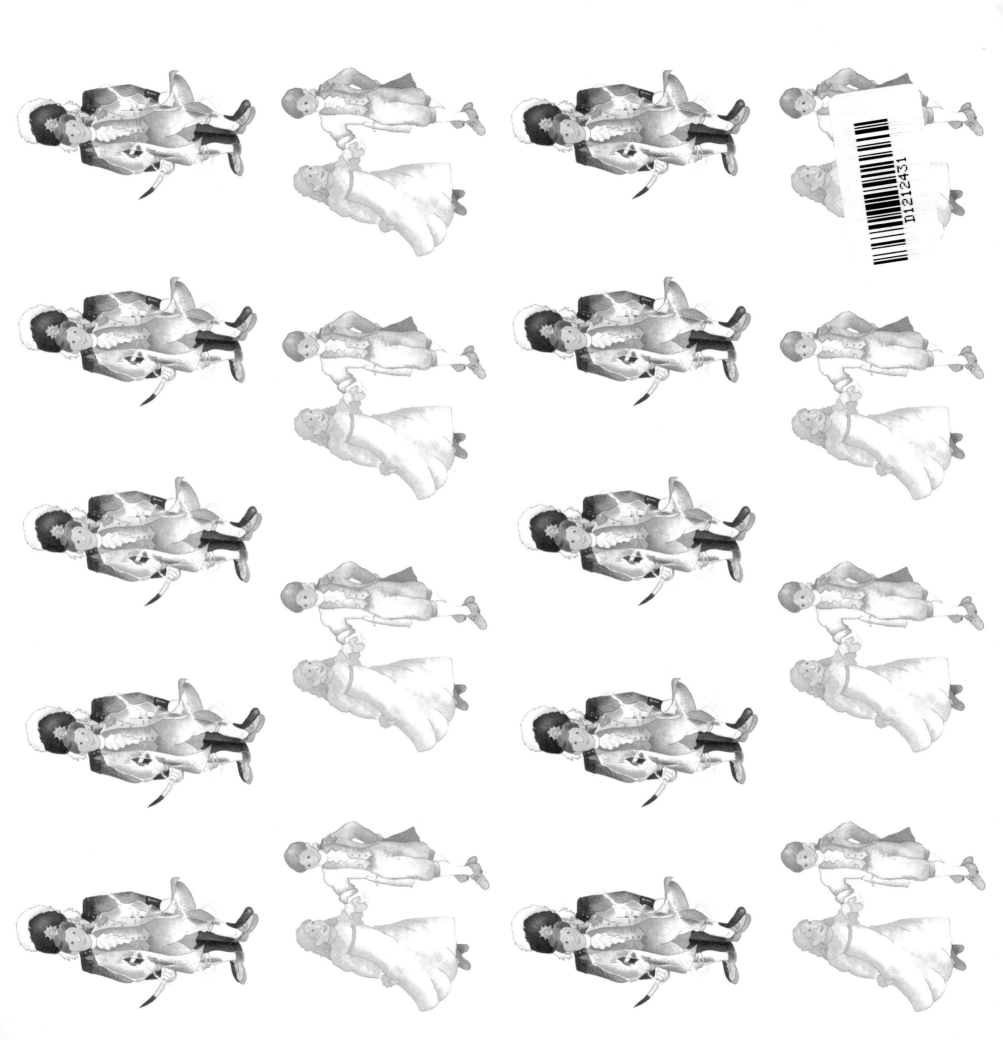

The Nutcracker

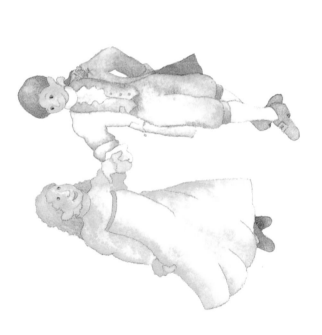

Adapted by Carin Dewhirst

Original Illustrations by Naomi Howland

FRIEDMAN/FAIRFAX
PUBLISHERS

A FRIEDMAN/FAIRFAX BOOK

A LIFE, TIMES & MUSIC™ BOOK
© 1997 Michael Friedman Publishing Group

Library of Congress Cataloging-in-Publication Data
Dewhirst, Carin.
The Nutcracker/Adapted by Carin Dewhirst; original illustrations by Naomi Howland

p. cm.

ISBN 1-56799-538-1 (hc)

1. Tchaikovsky, Peter Ilich, 1840-1893. Shchelkunchik.
2. Ballets—Stories, plots, etc.—Juvenile literature.
3. Nutcracker (Choreographic work) 1. Howland, Naomi.
ML3930.C4D49 1997
784.2'1556—dc21

97-10919
CIP
AC MN

Editors: Susan Lauzau, Celeste Sollod
Art Director/Designer: Jeff Batzli
Photography Editor: Deborah Bernhardt
Illustrator: Naomi Howland
Production Manager: Jeanne E. Hutter

Grateful acknowledgment is given to authors, publishers, and photographers for permission to reprint material. Every effort has been made to determine copyright owners of photographs and illustrations. In the case of any omissions, the publishers will be pleased to make suitable acknowledgments in future editions.

Color separations by HK Scanner Arts Int'l Ltd.
Printed in China by Leefung—Asco Printers Ltd.

10 9 8 7 6 5 4 3 2 1

For bulk purchases and special sales, please contact:
Friedman/Fairfax Publishers
Attention: Sales Department
15 West 26th Street
New York, New York 10010
212/685-6610   FAX 212/685-1307

Visit our website:
http://www.metrobooks.com

Dedication

To Grandma Betty, who baby-sat while I wrote, and to Blake, who inspired sweet thoughts
—C.D.

For my mother and father, with love
—N.P.H.

Credits

The Corbis-Bettmann Archive: 21
© Costas: 23, 24
© Paul Kolnick: 22

All performance photographs are *George Balanchine's The Nutcracker,*™ choreography © The George Balanchine Trust

Balanchine is a trademark of The George Balanchine Trust

Contents

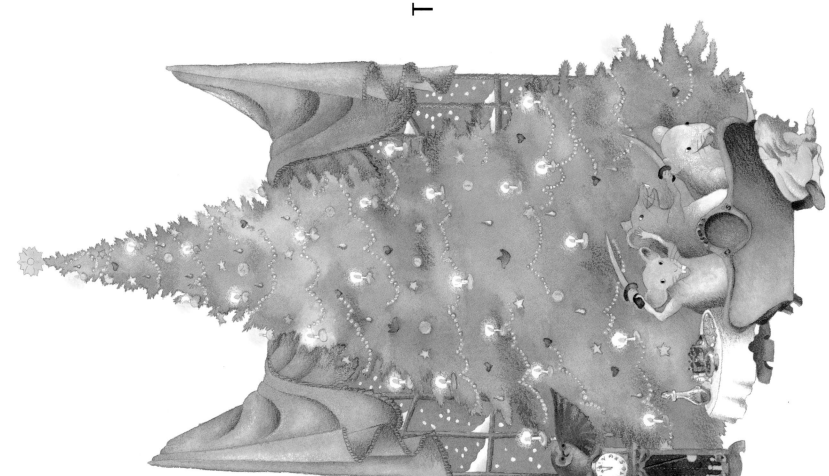

Introduction

WELCOME TO THE ENCHANTED WORLD OF *THE NUTCRACKER!* What an astonishing place it is. The world of *The Nutcracker* will surprise you, for the story seems quite, well, ordinary—at first. Two children, Clara and Fritz, are celebrating Christmas Eve with their friends when a mysterious visitor with magical powers arrives. Before you know it, an ordinary celebration becomes quite *extraordinary*. Clara and Fritz's house is transformed into an imaginative playground—toys come to life and dance, the Christmas tree grows to gigantic proportions, and huge mice clash swords with gingerbread soldiers. In a magic sleigh, Clara travels to the Land of Sweets and is entertained by confections of all sorts. All of this and more awaits you in *The Nutcracker*.

The story of the Nutcracker will amaze you and the music of Tchaikovsky will delight you. Perhaps you will want to march with toy soldiers, waltz with the Sugarplum Fairy, or spin and twirl with dancing snowflakes... it is up to you in the imaginative world of *The Nutcracker.* Welcome!

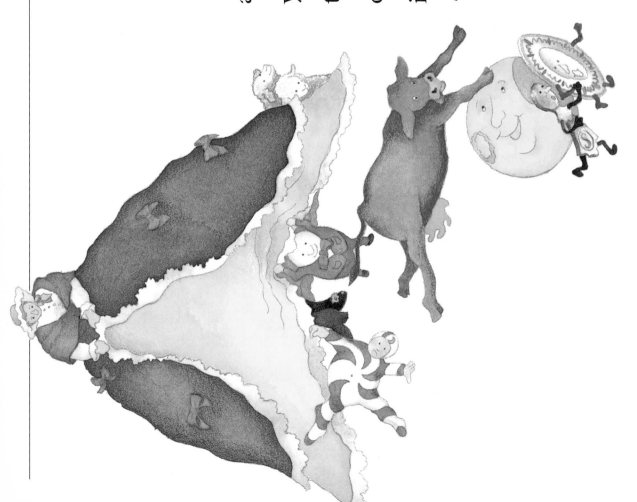

The Story of the
Nutcracker

It was Christmas Eve, and Fritz was trying to push aside his older sister, Clara, so he could peek through the keyhole of the parlor door. Behind the door, Fritz and Clara's parents were laughing and whispering as they arranged ornaments and placed presents under the Christmas tree. The children were not allowed in the parlor until the tree was ready, so Clara, Fritz, and their friends waited impatiently in the hallway until...at last! Clara and Fritz's father opened the parlor door and let them run into the room.

The children paused for a moment and stared in awe at the

Christmas tree. Tiny silver stars, golden moons, and brightly colored birds were suspended from each branch. Best of all, stacks and stacks of presents were crowded under the tree.

In no time, the floor was littered with torn wrapping paper and ribbons, and every single child was playing with a special toy. There were tiny tricycles, red wagons, miniature trains, lovely dolls, and furry stuffed animals.

Each gift was a dream come true, and the children danced around the room as they showed off their toys. In the midst of their festivity, they heard laughter and the rise and fall of voices from the hallway. The children realized that they were not the only ones having fun on this Christmas Eve.

6

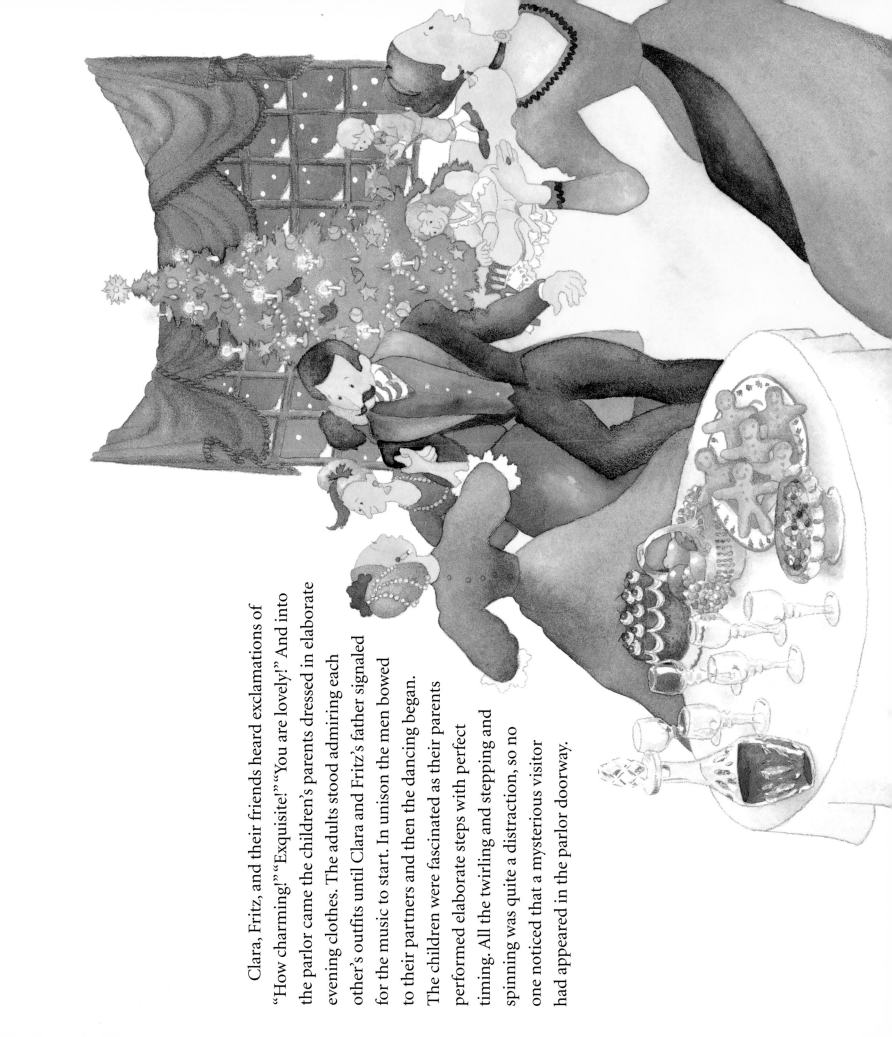

Clara, Fritz, and their friends heard exclamations of "How charming!" "Exquisite!" "You are lovely!" And into the parlor came the children's parents dressed in elaborate evening clothes. The adults stood admiring each other's outfits until Clara and Fritz's father signaled for the music to start. In unison the men bowed to their partners and then the dancing began. The children were fascinated as their parents performed elaborate steps with perfect timing. All the twirling and stepping and spinning was quite a distraction, so no one noticed that a mysterious visitor had appeared in the parlor doorway.

The man wore a long black cape and a tall hat. His face was quite wrinkled and a patch covered one eye. After several moments, Clara and Fritz saw the man. His unusual appearance frightened them both. To their surprise, their father stopped dancing and greeted the strange man warmly.

"Merry Christmas, Councilor Drosselmeyer!" their father said as he shook the stranger's hand. "So glad you could stop by. Clara, Fritz, come say hello to my dear friend."

Clara and Fritz hid behind their nanny's long, full skirt and refused to move.

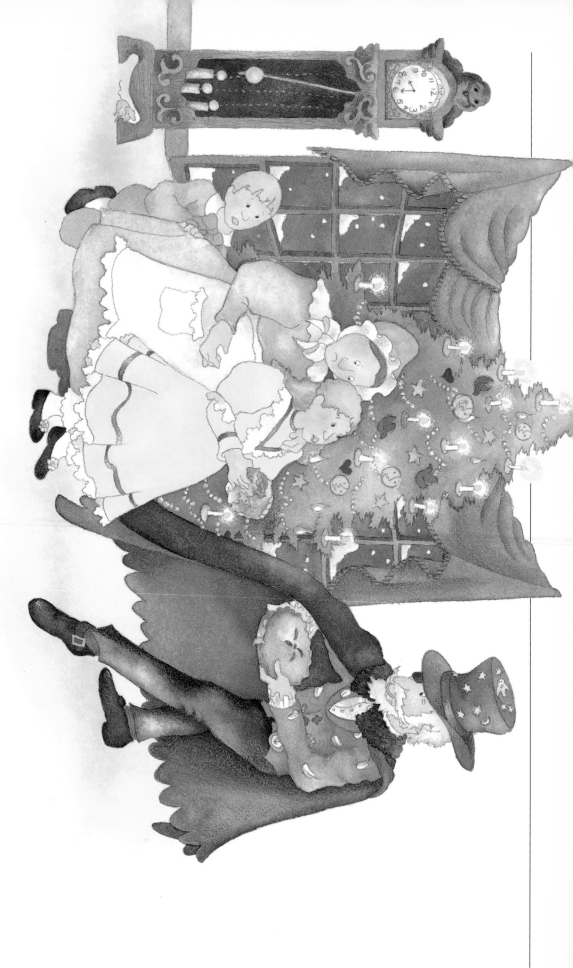

"Drosselmeyer, your odd looks have scared the wits out of my children! Show them some magic," Clara and Fritz's father suggested.

Drosselmeyer rummaged through several pockets. Finally he approached the children with his hands behind his back. With a flourish, Drosselmeyer gave a gift to Clara and then one to Fritz. Clara and Fritz's father began to chuckle and said, "Drosselmeyer, you are full of tricks. A pie for Fritz and a cabbage for Clara—what sort of gifts are those?"

"Those are magical gifts, my friend, as you shall see."

Drosselmeyer quickly lifted a hidden latch on Clara's cabbage and out popped a ballerina doll. Fritz's pie also had a hidden clasp; when the clasp was turned, a toy soldier jumped out. Drosselmeyer wound up the toys and they danced around and around. When the toys stopped, Clara and Fritz begged Drosselmeyer to make them dance again.

Their mother interrupted their pleas. "Clara and Fritz, it's time for bed; thank Councilor Drosselmeyer

and bid goodbye to your friends, as they are about to leave." Mother took the new toys and began to put them away.

"Oh, Mother," Clara begged. "May I take my doll with me, please?"

"Me too," Fritz pleaded.

"You will have plenty of time to play tomorrow. I will keep them safe until then."

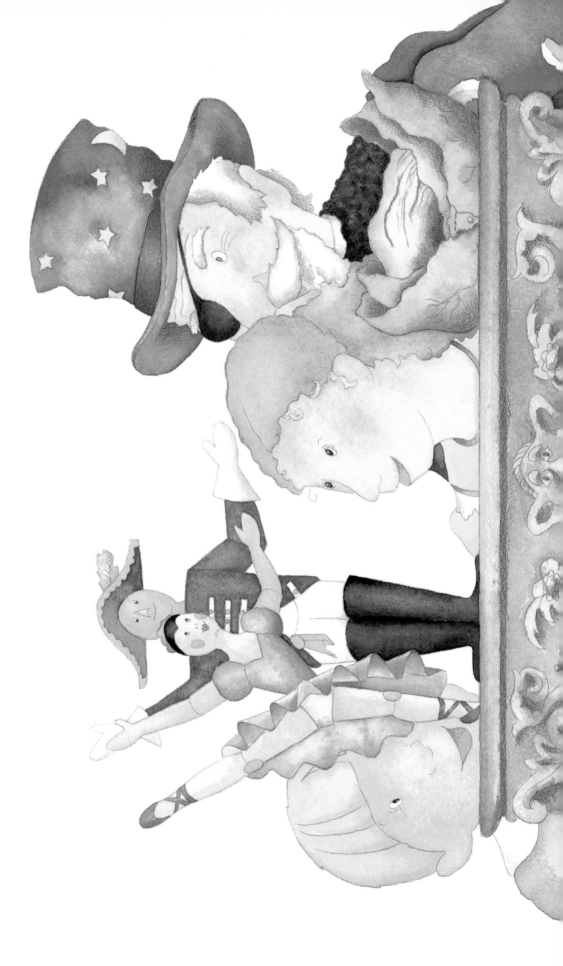

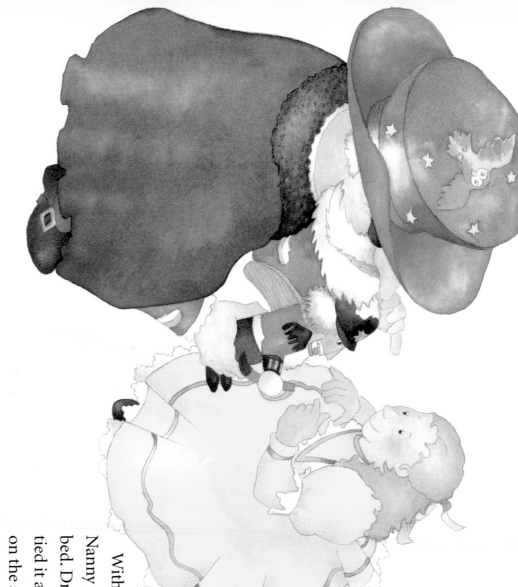

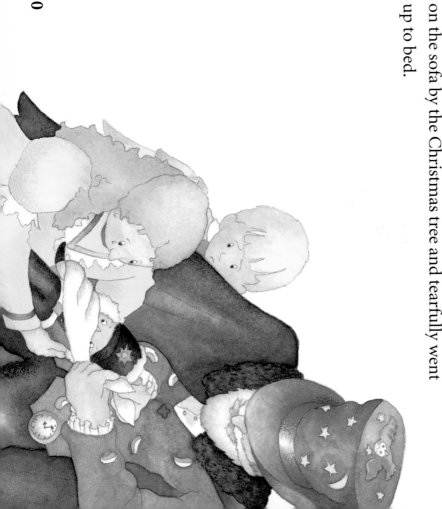

10

Both children pouted a bit, then Fritz reluctantly thanked Councilor Drosselmeyer. Clara attempted to speak but instead she burst into tears. Drosselmeyer reached into another deep pocket of his cape. From that pocket he produced an object wrapped in a silky scarf. He held it out toward Clara and slowly untied the scarf. There before her was a wooden nutcracker doll. The doll's jaw was very large and opened wide to hold nuts of all sizes. Clara's nutcracker wore an elegant military hat, was brightly painted, and even held a small sword in its hand—just like a real, live soldier. The moment Clara saw the nutcracker she loved it and knew it was unlike any other doll in the world.

Drosselmeyer showed Clara how to lift the handle at the back of the nutcracker's head… He placed a nut in the doll's mouth and neatly cracked it. Clara was happy again as Drosselmeyer handed her the doll. She cradled it in her arms.

All at once, Fritz jealously grabbed the doll and ran around the room. Before anyone could stop him, he took a huge nut and placed it in the nutcracker doll's mouth.

With a loud "CRACK!" the nut broke the doll's jaw. Nanny and Mother scolded Fritz and marched him off to bed. Drosselmeyer fashioned a bandage out of a scarf and tied it around the doll's jaw. Clara carefully placed the doll on the sofa by the Christmas tree and tearfully went up to bed.

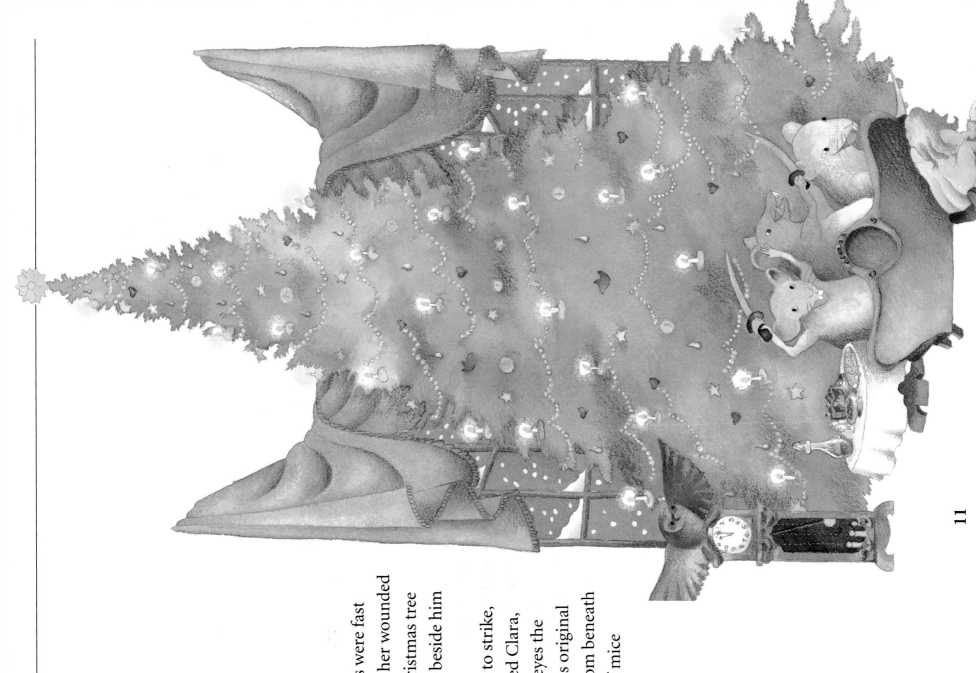

After the guests had gone and her parents were fast asleep, Clara tiptoed downstairs to check on her wounded doll. She gazed at him by the light of the Christmas tree for a moment, yawned widely, and lay down beside him on the sofa.

At midnight the grandfather clock began to strike, "BONG, BONG, BONG." The sounds startled Clara, but that was only the beginning. Before her eyes the Christmas tree grew and grew to ten times its original size. Mice the size of men came scurrying from beneath it. Clara hid behind the sofa as a battalion of mice gathered in formation behind their leader, the Mouse King.

Was Clara dreaming as she watched Fritz's toy soldiers and the plate of gingerbread men come to life and clash swords with the mice? Clara watched the battle and quickly realized that the gingerbread men and toy soldiers were no match for the mice. One by one, toy soldiers broke and gingerbread soldiers crumbled to the ground...just like cookies.

After a moment she saw that her nutcracker doll was no longer a small wooden toy. He still had a great wooden head, but he was now tall and strong.

To Clara the situation seemed hopeless, because the Nutcracker was surrounded by mice, but she did not know that the Nutcracker was a master swordsman. After several swift, sure strokes of the Nutcracker's sword, several mice went down. The other mice covered their faces and squealed in horror.

12

The evil Mouse King cornered the Nutcracker. He was about to attack the Nutcracker when Clara threw her slipper at the fierce Mouse King. Clara's slipper hit the Mouse King smartly on the head and he fainted. The other mice quickly dragged the Mouse King away.

Clara turned to the Nutcracker, but there in front of her was a real, live gallant Prince. The Prince explained, "You have saved my life and you have broken an evil spell. I am now a Prince again. As your reward I will take you to my kingdom. It is called the Land of Sweets because it is made of everything sweet. Would you be so kind as to accompany me?"

13

Clara agreed to his sweet offer in an instant. A fur-lined sleigh appeared and magically carried the Prince and Clara through the branches of the Christmas tree to a world beyond.

The sleigh glided under the evergreen boughs and arrived first at the Land of Snowflakes. The trees were dusted with snow from top to bottom and each tree branch was white and puffy. The Prince told Clara that fairies lived in the Land of Snowflakes. These fairies taught snowflakes to swirl and twirl properly.

Just then, the Snowflake Fairies began to dance for Clara and the Prince. Wearing short, puffy skirts and ice tiaras, the fairies waltzed and twirled around and around.

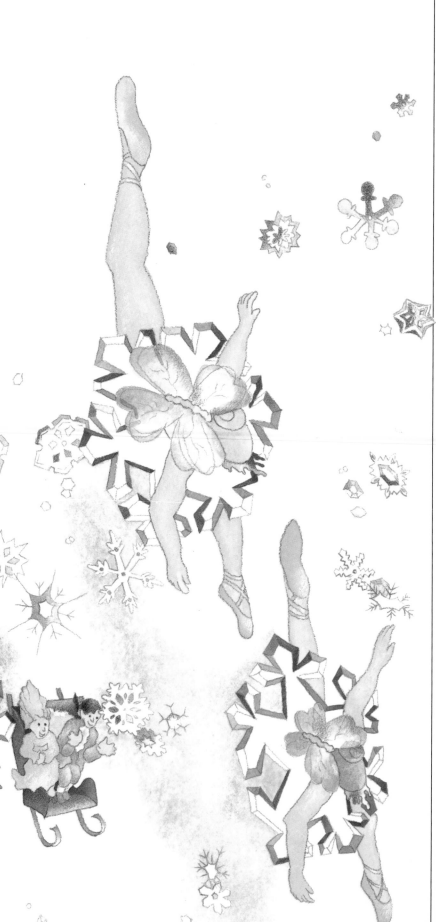

The Snowflake Fairies danced on the ground for a while, but since they had wings, they also flew above Clara and the Prince. Clara watched them dance across the sky. The Snowflake Fairies flew ahead of the sleigh and guided it safely to the Land of Sweets.

Clara knew they were approaching the Prince's kingdom, the Land of Sweets, because the air began to smell sweeter and sweeter. Soon Clara could see the tall stone walls of the Prince's castle. A moat filled with melted caramel surrounded it. The sleigh rode over a drawbridge made of a slab of dark chocolate.

The sleigh came to rest in the courtyard of the Prince's castle. Clara thought that the walls glittered as if they were sugarcoated; then she remembered that this was the Land of Sweets, so everything *was* dusted with sugar! She was thrilled by the lollipop window panes, gingerbread walls, and pillars made from stacks of gumdrops. But what thrilled her the most was the Prince. As she gazed at him, he rose to his feet and recounted all that Clara had done for him.

15

He began by describing the huge Mouse King with his sharp teeth and battalion of mice soldiers. All the subjects in the kingdom covered their eyes and cowered when he told how the gingerbread soldiers crumbled during the attack of the giant mice. They gasped when they heard about the Mouse King cornering the Prince and threatening him with a very sharp sword. But when the Prince came to the part where brave Clara threw her slipper at the Mouse King, the whole crowd cheered and clapped.

A beautiful fairy stepped forward wearing a gown of spun sugar. This was the Sugarplum Fairy and she was in charge of all the fairies in the land. The Sugarplum Fairy immediately ordered a luscious banquet of sweets and had it set before Clara.

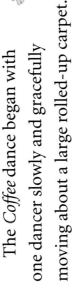

The *Coffee* dance began with one dancer slowly and gracefully moving about a large rolled-up carpet. To everyone's surprise, when the carpet was unrolled, out came another dancer! Together they performed the smoothest, most elegant dance Clara had ever seen.

After the *Coffee* dance ended, the fairy shouted "Tea!" Dancers wearing bright, shiny jackets danced in on the tips of their toe shoes. These dancers wore Chinese costumes because it is said that tea originated in China.

Next, dancers in Russian costume leaped across the stage. Wearing smart red jackets, tall hats, and shiny leather boots, the dancers kicked their legs in front of them as they squatted close to the floor.

Two fairies escorted Clara to a throne, where she sat right next to the Prince. When everyone was seated, the Sugarplum Fairy clapped her hands and the music started. A fairy announced, "To honor brave Clara, let the entertainment begin! Chocolate! Dance!"

Two dancers appeared in front of Clara and the Prince. These two dancers represented chocolate, so they wore costumes of deep brown velvet. The couple performed a Spanish dance called a bolero.

The performance of *Chocolate* was short and fast-paced. Before Clara knew it, it was over and she heard a fairy shout, "Coffee!"

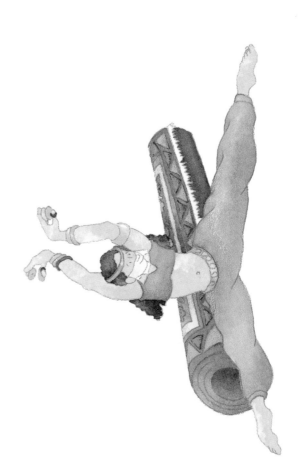

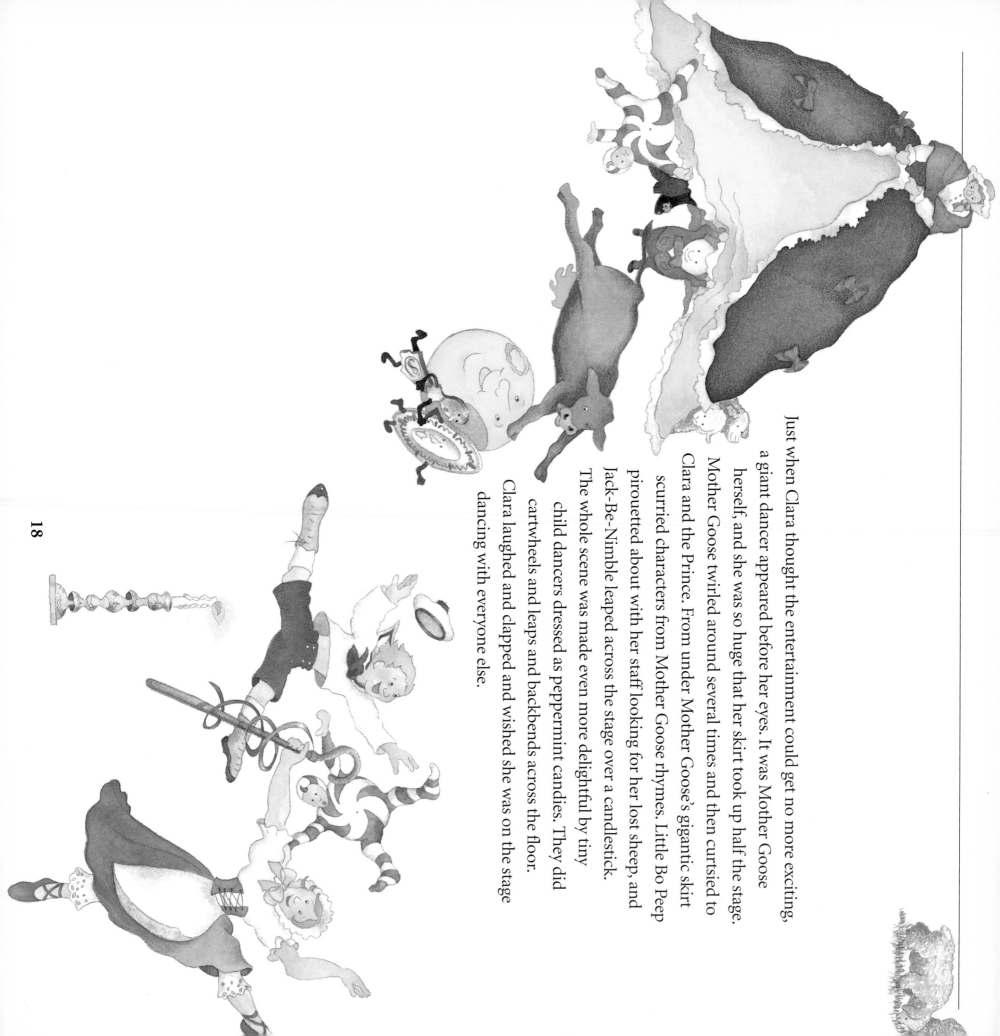

Just when Clara thought the entertainment could get no more exciting, a giant dancer appeared before her eyes. It was Mother Goose herself, and she was so huge that her skirt took up half the stage. Mother Goose twirled around several times and then curtsied to Clara and the Prince. From under Mother Goose's gigantic skirt scurried characters from Mother Goose rhymes. Little Bo Peep pirouetted about with her staff looking for her lost sheep, and Jack-Be-Nimble leaped across the stage over a candlestick.

The whole scene was made even more delightful by tiny child dancers dressed as peppermint candies. They did cartwheels and leaps and backbends across the floor.

Clara laughed and clapped and wished she was on the stage dancing with everyone else.

18

Clara was sorry to see Mother Goose and her children leave the dance floor, but before her eyes the stage filled with dancing flowers. Lilies, roses, pansies, tulips, daisies, violets, and poppies waltzed around and around and around until Clara was almost dizzy.

After a moment the Prince took Clara's hand and led her from her throne. There among the flowers they danced, as did the Sugarplum Fairy and her Cavalier. Clara closed her eyes and wished that she could stay with her Prince forever and ever....

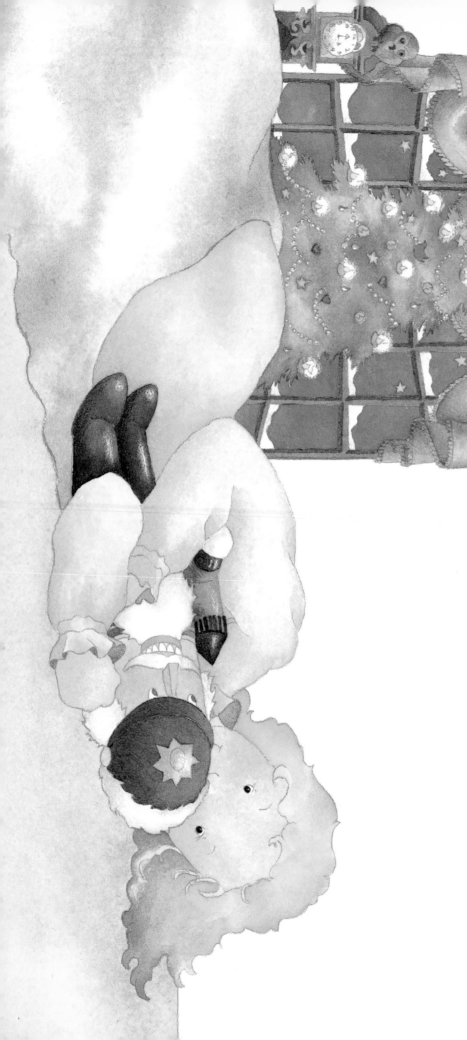

The grandfather clock began to strike, "BONG, BONG, BONG." The sounds startled Clara. She opened her eyes and found she was hugging her nutcracker doll. Where was she? Where was the Land of Sweets? "It could not have been a dream," she thought. She looked at the nutcracker doll. By the light of the Christmas tree she saw that the scarf bandage was gone and that the doll had been repaired. Clara smiled and tiptoed quietly back up to bed.

About the Composer

Peter Ilyich Tchaikovsky

Peter Ilyich Tchaikovsky (pronounced "chy-KAWF-skee") was born on May 7, 1840, in a village called Votkinsk six hundred miles (960 kilometers) east of Moscow. Tchaikovsky's mother sang folk songs, popular arias, and contemporary romantic songs. His family owned a mechanical organ (CD players had not yet been invented), which played songs automatically when metal cylinders were placed inside it. The Tchaikovskys' organ played Wolfgang Amadeus Mozart's *Don Giovanni*, among other classical pieces.

Mozart's music impressed and inspired young Peter Tchaikovsky. When Tchaikovsky began writing his own compositions, listeners could hear Mozartlike passages in his work. One piece in particular, Tchaikovsky's Suite no. 4, was a tribute to Mozart and was called *Mozartiana.*

In addition to Mozart's music, the folk songs that Tchaikovsky's mother had sung to him influenced his own work. Some of his pieces—such as the two piano pieces of his Opus 1 and his String Quartet no. 1, Opus 11—contain melodies similar to the familiar folk tunes of his childhood.

Tchaikovsky was introduced to various forms of music as a child and began taking piano lessons at age five, but it was not until he was an adult that he devoted his life to becoming a musician. When Tchaikovsky was ten years old, his parents sent him to the School of Jurisprudence to train as a lawyer. He studied there until he was nineteen years old, but during that time he also continued his music lessons. He helped the school's choir director, studied harmony, and took piano lessons.

When Tchaikovsky graduated from the School of Jurisprudence, he went to work for the government as a civil servant in the Ministry of Justice. According to letters Tchaikovsky wrote to his sister Sacha, he felt that he was not a very good civil servant, yet he was also con-

cerned that it was too late to start a career as a musician.

However, in 1862 Tchaikovsky finally devoted his life to music. He quit his job and entered the Saint Petersburg Conservatory. When he graduated, he won a silver medal for a cantata he had written.

After studying at the Saint Petersburg Conservatory, Tchaikovsky taught music theory for eleven years at the Moscow Conservatory. During that time he composed his famous *Swan Lake* ballet, four operas, three symphonies, and many shorter works. Tchaikovsky's popularity began to grow and he formed friendships with other important Russian composers.

Tchaikovsky's achievements were recognized all over the world. In 1891 he went to the United States to conduct at the opening night of a music hall that would later be named Carnegie Hall. He was honored in France and England with special awards. By the time he died in 1893, he was so important in Russia that Tsar Alexander III allowed him to have a state funeral, an honor reserved for very few.

Concertgoers continue to enjoy Tchaikovsky's music. One of Tchaikovsky's important contributions was to the development of ballet music. Tchaikovsky wrote ballet music that added to the feeling and meaning of the dance. You can experience this yourself as you listen to *The Nutcracker.*

A Listener's Guide to *The Nutcracker*

The first step to enjoying *The Nutcracker* is to sit back and listen to the entire ballet. Do not worry about following the story and the music together; just concentrate on the beautiful melodies. After you have listened to the CD once or twice, read the plot summary that follows so that you will know what is happening in the story.

Track 1: Overture

An overture is an introduction and a summary. It is an introduction because it comes before the other sections of a larger piece of music—usually the first movement of a classical symphony, though in *The Nutcracker* it comes before a ballet. An overture is similar to a summary because it often contains tunes, melodies, or rhythms that are also in other parts of the piece.

> After you have listened to the entire ballet, go back to the overture to find melodies that were in other parts of the piece.

Act I

Track 2: Decoration of the Christmas Tree

The music echoes the busy preparations for Christmas. The adults are decorating the tree and the children are marching about. Finally the children run into the parlor to see the Christmas tree, and the sight of it delights them.

Track 3: March

The children receive their presents and then dance about joyfully to some of the most famous and memorable melodies of *The Nutcracker*.

Track 4: Children's Gallup and Entry of the Parents

The children's dance is interrupted by the entrance of the parents in costume.

Track 5: Arrival of Drosselmeyer

The music abruptly changes to indicate Drosselmeyer's appearance in the parlor doorway. He scares Clara and Fritz, then delights them by making their toys dance.

Track 6: Grandfather's Dance

The children want to play with their new toys but Mother sends them to bed. Clara cries and Drosselmeyer gives her the nutcracker doll, which Fritz breaks.

Track 7: Clara and the Nutcracker

Clara creeps downstairs to check on her nutcracker doll. The Christmas tree becomes gigantic and huge mice fill the room.

Track 8: The Battle

The sounds of the drum, flute, and horn create the feeling of a battle as the mice and gingerbread soldiers fight. Clara throws her slipper at the Mouse King. Listen for a change in the music that indicates that the Nutcracker has turned into a Prince. He and Clara glide through the branches of the Christmas tree.

Track 9: In the Pine Forest

The strong sounds and beat of the battle scene melt away to dreamy melodies played with a harp and other stringed instruments. To this music, Clara and the Prince travel through a wintry landscape.

Track 10: Waltz of the Snowflakes

Clara and the Prince watch the Snowflake Fairies dance. This track is unique because of the use of voices and instruments.

Act II

Divertissement

Clara and the Prince arrive in the Land of Sweets and the Prince describes Clara's brave deed. The Sugar Plum Fairy orders dancers to celebrate. This section is called a *divertissement*, which means amusement. A divertissement is usually made up of a group of dances or songs. The six dances of *The Nutcracker* divertissement contain some of the best-known melodies from the ballet.

Track 11: Chocolate—Spanish Dance
Chocolate is a Spanish dance—listen for castanets.

Track 12: Coffee—Arabian Dance
Coffee is an Arabian dance and features the tambourine.

Track 13: Tea—Chinese Dance
Tea is a Chinese dance. Can you hear the glockenspiel? It's a percussion instrument that looks like two xylophones side by side.

Track 14: Trepak—Russian Dance
A *trepak* is a Russian dance done to a simple beat.

Track 15: Dance of the Reed Flutes
This dance is also called the dance of the toy flutes.

Track 16: Mother Gigone and the Puppets
Mother Gigone is another name for Mother Goose. She is always accompanied by her children or puppets.

Track 17: Waltz of the Flowers
In the Land of Sweets, even the flowers dance for Clara and the Prince. These flowers perform a waltz.

Track 18: Dance of the Sugarplum Fairy
The Sugarplum Fairy and her partner dance a *pas de deux*, or "steps for two."

The Sugarplum Fairy's dance

A *pas de deux* is often the main part or center-piece of a ballet and is used to show strong emotions, such as love or joy. The Sugarplum Fairy's *pas de deux* reminds the audience of the love Clara has for the Prince. Remember to listen for the celesta during the Sugarplum Fairy's dance.

Track 19: Waltz Finale
The ballet ends with everyone waltzing.

Track 20: Apotheosis
Apotheosis means the act of becoming divine or godlike. In this final part of *The Nutcracker*, Clara and the Prince travel heavenward in an enchanted sleigh.

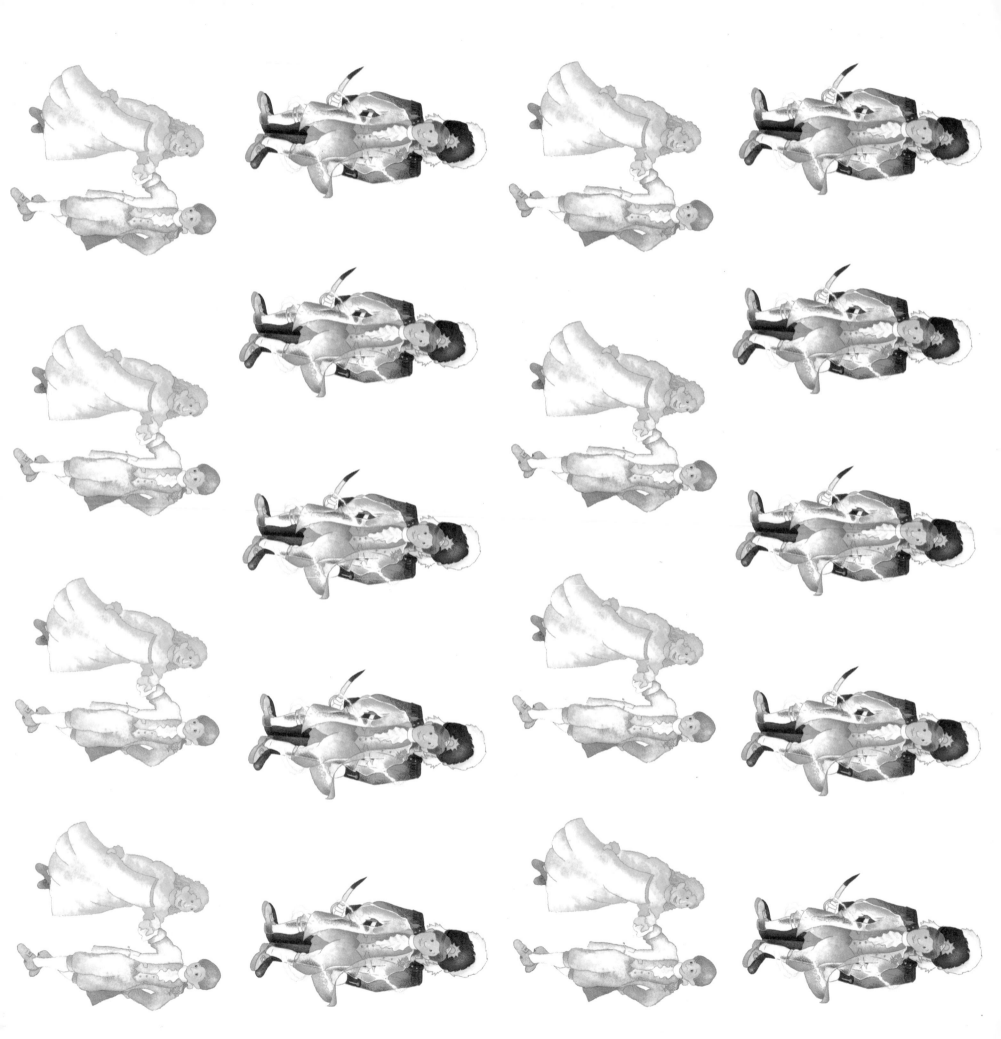